MISSAUKEE DISTRICT LIBRARY

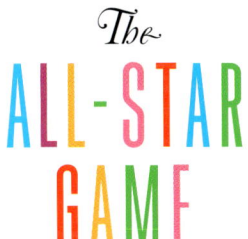

The ALL-STAR GAME

Published by Creative Education, Inc.
123 South Broad Street, Mankato, MN 56001

Designed by Rita Marshall with the help of Thomas Lawton

Cover illustration by Rob Day, Lance Hidy Associates

Copyright © 1993 by Creative Education, Inc.
All rights reserved. No part of this book may be reproduced in any form without written permission from the publisher.

Photography by Allsport, Mel Bailey, Bettmann Archive, Duomo, FPG International, National Baseball Library, Sports Illustrated (John Iacono, John Hanlon, Neil Leifer, George Long, V. J. Lovero, Donald Modra, Mickey Picdger, Jerry Wachter), SportsLight (Steven Goldstein), Wide World Photos

Printed in the United States

Library of Congress Cataloging-in-Publication Data

Potts, Steve, 1956–
The All-Star Game / Steve Potts.
Summary: Describes memorable moments in the All-Star Baseball Game, the midsummer matchup between the best players in the American and National Leagues that began in 1933.
ISBN 0-88682-537-7
1. All-Star Baseball Game—History—Juvenile literature. [1. All-Star Baseball Game—History. 2. Baseball—History.] I. Title.
GV878.P68   1992
796.357'648—dc20

92-4111
CIP
AC

The ALL-STAR GAME

STEVE POTTS

CREATIVE EDUCATION INC.

President John F. Kennedy tossed out the first ball in the 1962 All-Star Game at Washington's D.C. Stadium, and the game was on. More than forty-five thousand fans settled down to watch a pitching duel between Jim Bunning and Camilio Pascaul for the American League and Don Drysdale and Juan Marichal for the National League.

The first five innings were scoreless. By the eighth inning, though, the National League had a slim lead of 2-1. Then Los Angeles Dodger Maury Wills strode to the plate.

A Washington native, Wills responded to the crowd's cheers with a warm smile. The fans were eager to see if this hometown boy would live up to his reputation as baseball's fastest man. With all that speed, Wills was one of the sport's most exciting base runners.

Wills leaned into the pitch, swung hard, and fired a single off his bat. Even before the crowd could hear the crack of the bat, Wills was dashing down the baseline to

Maury Wills slides.

Pitchers Carl Hubbell (left) and Lefty Grove faced each other in the 1936 contest.

first. Would he stop there? His National League team was only ahead by one run. Would Maury Wills, with his legendary legs, put on a base-running exhibition?

THE MIGHTY SULTAN

Although the sport of baseball is over a century old, the midsummer matchup between the American and National leagues did not begin until 1933. Unlike the World Series, which pits the best AL and NL teams against each other at season's end, the July contest pits the best players in each league against one another. This competition between baseball's best makes the All-Star Game one of the year's most exciting events.

The first All-Star Game was held on July 6, 1933, at Chicago's Comiskey Park. It was a battle some writers called "The Game of the Century." Connie Mack (American League) and John McGraw (National League), both already baseball legends, managed their league's stars. And what stars! National League standouts included Lon Warneke, Gabby Hartnett, Carl Hubbell, and a pitcher who struck fear into batters' hearts, "Wild Bill" Hallahan. Their American League opponents included Babe Ruth, fellow Yankee Lou Gehrig, Jimmie Foxx, Wes Ferrell, and "Lefty" Gomez. The National League, the loser in the World Series five of the last six years, was anxious to get its revenge during the midseason contest.

Of all these baseball stars, none held the crowd's attention like the legendary Babe Ruth. At thirty-eight years old, with fading eyes and weakened stamina, Ruth wasn't expected to do much in the first All-Star Game. But the crowd applauded wildly for old Babe, the man who had already entered the record books for his powerful bat and amazing fielding.

Jose Canseco's mighty swing.

When Babe Ruth walked onto Comiskey Field's diamond that day in 1933, he had already seen twenty years in the major leagues. "The Sultan of Swat," as sportswriters nicknamed Babe Ruth, began his career in 1914 as a left-handed pitcher with the Boston Red Sox. Although he was a good pitcher, he was a great batter, something his Red Sox coach noticed. By 1918, Ruth had become an outfielder.

The versatile Bo Jackson.

Two modern-day giants: Andre Dawson (left) and Kirby Puckett.

In what had to be one of baseball's all-time best deals, the New York Yankees bought Ruth from the Red Sox in January 1920. Ruth rewarded the Yankees with an amazing fifty-four homers in his first year with the team. His .376 batting average quickly established him as one of the game's premier sluggers. The next year Ruth hit fifty-nine home runs, with a .378 batting average and 171 runs batted in. His powerful bat helped the Yankees win eleven American League pennants and eight World Series championships during the 1920s and 1930s.

Detroit All-Star Chet Lemon.

Few players, though, can keep up such a pace for twenty years. By 1933, Babe Ruth was past his prime. Formerly muscular at 205 pounds, he was now sluggish at 240 pounds. His reflexes had slowed, his batting eye had faded, and he wheezed and pulled in deep breaths after chasing fly balls in the outfield. "Babe can still hit—no doubt about it—but he looks slow," one Chicago sportswriter observed.

The first All-Star Game began on a sour note for Ruth. In the first inning, "Wild Bill" Hallahan caused the first batter to ground out, walked the second, then faced the mighty Ruth. After the crowd's cheers quieted, Ruth stepped to the plate, faced three straight pitches, and struck out.

Boston's Roger Clemens.

Ruth paid close attention to his opponent, however, and was determined to get his revenge on Hallahan. He got his chance in the third inning, with the American League holding a slim 1-0 lead. Stepping defiantly to the plate and scuffing his feet in the dirt, Ruth rubbed the bat between his hands. With Charlie Gehringer on base on a walk, Ruth had a chance to drive in two more runs to boost his team's lead.

"Wild Bill" Hallahan.

Ruth stepped into the batter's box under Hallahan's steady gaze. Winding up, Hallahan angled a curve ball across the plate for his first pitch and fired a fastball for the second for a 1-1 count. Ruth stepped outside the batter's box, stooped over, and, after mashing some dirt between his hands, dusted them off on his pants. He was ready for the third pitch. The fans edged forward in their seats.

Hallahan turned his head, gazed around the diamond, and took in the silent crowd. He threw his third pitch. Ruth waited a split second, then leaned into the pitch.

The remarkable Babe.

With a powerful swing, his bat met the ball. Spectators leaped to their feet at the sound of the crack. Shading their eyes, the fans watched the ball's progress. It shot into the right-field bleachers for a two-run homer. Ruth dropped his bat, tipped his cap, and lumbered around the bases. His teammates clapped the Sultan of Swat on the back as he walked into the dugout. The American League now had a 3-0 lead.

The crowd's enthusiasm lessened after the sixth inning, however, when Babe Ruth made a disappointing error. Ruth stood in right field when National League pitcher

Fans scramble for the ball.

Lon Warneke came to the plate. Unlike most pitchers, Warneke could hit, compiling a .300 average during the 1933 season. Warneke leaned under AL pitcher Alvin Crowder's pitch, ripped a short fly ball into right field, and began his dash to first base. To the fans, it looked like an easy catch for Ruth. Wheezing and puffing, Ruth pushed toward the falling ball, but it fell several feet in front of his glove, bounced, and rolled to the bleacher wall. What should have been a single became a triple, and a grinning Warneke stood on third.

Like Warneke, pitching ace Dwight Gooden is a good hitter.

Willie Mays, another All-Star hero.

A Chicago writer, seeing Ruth's fumbling fielding, said, "Toldja. That Ruth runs like an old lady . . . any half-decent fielder would have put away that fly ball with no trouble." To add insult to injury, Warneke the pitcher struck Ruth out at the bottom of the sixth.

Ruth's poor performance upset him, and not even the glory of his two-run homer could ease his anger. He was determined to make it up to the fans—and to himself.

By the eighth inning the National League was threatening to come from behind and win. With two out and one man on first, Cincinnati's Chick Hafey, a powerful hitter and the 1931 NL batting champ, came to the plate. On the first pitch, Hafey swung squarely, smashing the ball deep toward the right-field bleachers. The crowd peered toward right field and quieted. That was Ruth's territory, and there seemed no way the aging fielder could save his league from a two-run homer.

But Ruth responded instinctively, his years of training erasing the doubts of age. He turned when the bat cracked, ran back to the right-field wall, and looked up to see the ball falling. He leaned against the wall. Ruth knew he had only one chance. He would have to jump.

And what a jump it was. He sprang high into the air, all 240 pounds of him, and caught the ball in his glove's webbing. The force knocked him into the wall. He slid down, then stood up. When he rose, the ball was still in his glove. He had robbed Hafey and the National League of a homer!

Friendships are renewed at the All-Star Game.

A few lucky fans receive autographs from the stars.

The stunned crowd slowly rose as one mass and began cheering. Some spectators shook their heads in amazement. Ruth had proved his critics wrong. With a two-run homer and a miraculous catch, Babe Ruth reminded fans of why he was the game's greatest player. That warm summer day marked one of his personal triumphs, and one of the All-Star Game's greatest moments.

The final score: American League 4; National League 2.

Chicago baseball fans watch a game at Wrigley Field from a nearby apartment.

BOSTON'S MIGHTY BAT

In 1936, a year after Babe Ruth retired, a cocky young hitter named Ted Williams joined the San Diego Padres minor league team. At first no one expected him to last a year, much less be compared one day with the great Babe Ruth. As one critic remembered, Ted Williams was "perhaps the worst outfielder ever to wear a glove." He also had a famous temper. Once, when a ground ball rolled between his legs and fans booed him, he talked back to the bleachers for the rest of the game and let more fly balls fall around him. On one memorable occasion after he had moved to Minneapolis, he went into the locker room after going hitless for three games and tore up every uniform and towel he found.

A hitless Williams was an oddity, however, and fans forgave his antics because of his great performance at the plate. When he came to the majors in 1939 and signed with the Red Sox, he continued both his powerful hitting and his frequent temper tantrums. After missing one fly ball, Williams picked it up and tossed it into the stands at the booing fans. But he also batted an amazing .401 in 1941. Fans missed his antics—and his batting—when he joined the Navy as a Marine flyer during World War II.

Boston powerhouse Wade Boggs.

Designated hitter Alvin Davis.

The war changed Ted Williams; when the twenty-eight-year-old came back to Boston in 1946, he was a new man. Instead of practicing alone and being booed by Red Sox fans, Williams joined his teammates in tough workouts and ignored the fans' heckling. Soon the jeers turned to cheers as the 1946 Red Sox cinched the American League pennant during the season's early months. Nothing could stop Williams and the Sox, it seemed.

The 1946 All-Star Game was held at Boston's Fenway Park. No All-Star Game had been played the previous year because of the war, and hometown fans were anxious to see their heroes—especially the top five AL sluggers, all of whom wore the Red Sox uniform: Dom DiMaggio, Johnny Pesky, Bobby Doerr, Rudy York, and, of course, the much mellower Ted Williams.

Excited about the event, Williams had two new bats made especially for him to use during the All-Star Game. With reporters looking on, he lifted one bat before the game, stared at the wood grain, and said, with a slight smile, "This bat really has some wood in it. They ought to ride off this today."

Red Sox 1946 All-Stars (from left): Rudy York, Ted Williams, and Bobby Doerr.

A modern-day pitching legend, Nolan Ryan.

He wasn't kidding. His blistering bats put Ted Williams and the 1946 All-Star Game in the record books. With one walk and four hits in five trips to the plate, Williams compiled a perfect record. His walk came in the first inning when National League pitcher Claude Passeau was on the mound. Passeau must have shivered when he saw the man sportswriters called "Titanic Ted." He pitched carefully to Williams, and breathed a sigh of relief when the slugger walked. Unfortunately for the National League, that was the last time at bat that Williams didn't get a hit. Williams ripped a home run and a single against Kirby Higbe, and singled against Ewell Blackwell. But his greatest moment came in the eighth inning, when he faced Truett "Rip" Sewell with two men already on base.

Sewell had a famous pitch he called the ephus ball, after an old gambling term. Sportswriters called it the blooper. No one had ever hit a home run off this pitch. Sewell lobbed the ball to the plate, where it looked to batters like a large, slow sphere just waiting to be smacked. Sewell added a clever backspin, however, and if it was hit at all, the ball usually ended up in a fielder's glove for an easy out.

With three hits already, Williams had no intention of becoming Sewell's next victim. He ambled confidently to the plate. Sewell bent over, stared at Williams, and fired his opening pitch. The first blooper was just out of the strike zone. Williams swung and missed. The crowd groaned.

Ted Williams at the plate.

Pages 20–21: Clowning around before the 1990 All-Star Game.

Then Williams remembered teammate Bill Dickey's advice: The way to hit the ephus ball, Dickey insisted, was to advance a step or two as it came toward you. With that in mind, Williams stepped into the batter's box. Sewell wound up, extended his arm, and delivered a second ephus pitch. Carefully watching the ball's course, Williams hopped toward the pitch and swung. The crack of the bat echoed through the stadium. Williams walloped the ball 380 feet into the right-field bullpen for a three-run homer. Sewell shook his head in wonder as Williams, grinning for all he was worth, followed his two teammates around the bases.

In a 12-0 shutout, Williams drove in five runs on four hits, two of them home runs. Losing National League manager Charlie Grimm praised Williams's performance as "one of the greatest one-man batting shows I've ever seen." Sportswriters who had branded Williams as overrated now had nothing but praise for "The Boston Kid." And the 1946 contest went into the record books as one of Ted Williams's triumphs and a great All-Star Game.

Andre Dawson (left) gets some batting advice from Darryl Strawberry and Dwight Gooden.

THE AMAZING DR. K

The All-Star Game has seen great hitting from the likes of Babe Ruth and Ted Williams, but it has also witnessed some of baseball's best pitching. At the 1984 All-Star Game in San Francisco's Candlestick Park, baseball fans saw a stunning performance by the youngest player ever to appear in an All-Star Game. His name was Dwight Gooden, and he was a nineteen-year-old pitcher for the New York Mets.

Gooden's appearance as a rookie in an All-Star Game made news by itself, but the strikeout record he and Fernando Valenzuela set was even more impressive, especially considering the windy conditions at Candlestick Park that night. Gooden also pitched at the worst time of day. The game started at 5:40 P.M. for eastern television viewers, a time when, as George Brett said, "It wasn't dark and it wasn't light—somewhere in between."

1990 National League All-Stars Roberto Alomar, Ryne Sandberg, and Bobby Bonilla.

All-Star pitcher Don Drysdale, winner of 1962's Cy Young award.

But if anyone was prepared to deal with such conditions, it was Dwight Gooden. From the time he began walking, Dwight seemed a natural for baseball. His father coached a local semipro team, the Tampa Dodgers, in Dwight's hometown of Tampa, Florida. Dwight was just three years old when his father began tossing balls to him, and he joined his first team at the age of eight. At first "Dr. K," as Dwight was nicknamed, wanted to play outfield, like his hero, Al Kaline, but he soon changed to pitching.

His first years as a pitcher weren't his easiest. When he was fourteen his temper flared after losing a game. "I thought I was never supposed to lose or give up hits," Gooden admitted. "I gave up something like eight runs in one and one-third innings, banged my hand against a wall, and fractured my wrist."

Dwight Gooden.

Eventually Gooden settled down and became, at age seventeen, the first pick for the Mets in the June 1982 amateur draft. In his 1984 opener in the Astrodome, when he pitched before his parents, he demonstrated the coolness under pressure that marks a winner. "I don't ever doubt myself. I don't feel any pressure," he said. "Of course, I hear the crowds; I just try to stay calm, follow my game plan, and not overthrow."

NL stars Kevin Mitchell, Darryl Strawberry, and Ryne Sandberg.

Fellow All-Stars Ozzie Smith and Roberto Alomar.

That coolness soon led to some impressive statistics: Dwight Gooden finished his first season with 276 strikeouts, surpassing a rookie record that had stood since 1955. He pitched three shutouts and compiled a 17-9 win-loss record, with a 2.60 earned run average in 218 innings. He was also named the NL Rookie of the Year, and his strong performance won him a spot on the All-Star team.

The 1990 All-Star Game pitted AL manager Tony LaRussa against NL manager Roger Craig.

Behind the scenes at the All-Star Game, Gooden was pleased to meet eighty-one-year-old Carl Hubbell, whose All-Star record of five straight strikeouts had stood for fifty years. Hubbell had been chosen to toss out the first ball that night. It was fifty years to the day since he had set his long-standing record. But that record was soon to be broken.

Fernando Valenzuela entered the game in the fourth inning and fanned all three batters he faced. Gooden came to the mound in the fifth inning. He quickly dispatched Detroit Tigers Lance Parrish and Chet Lemon. Then Seattle Mariner Alvin Davis stepped to the plate. Gooden was well aware of the pressure on him. If he fanned Davis, he and Valenzuela would have six consecutive strikeouts. They would beat Hubbell's record of five straight strikeouts and equal an All-Star feat accomplished only four times before: striking out the only three batters faced in an inning.

Gooden picked up the ball, nervously rolling it around in his glove as Davis stepped up to the batter's box. Davis was nervous as well. This was his first appearance in an All-Star game, too, and he was well aware of what was at stake for Gooden. The crowd grew quiet.

This contest between two newcomers ended with Gooden's last pitch. Davis rubbed his hands on his pant legs, slipped his bat between his hands, assumed his batting stance, and focused on Gooden. Gooden bent over, wound up, and released his pitch. A high, hard fastball rushed toward Davis. He swung—air rushed past his bat—and the ball smacked into the catcher's mitt. Davis had struck out!

Seattle Mariner Alvin Davis.

Fernando Valenzuela winds up for the pitch.

the high, hard beater and there's no one I can compare him with. There's certainly no nineteen-year-old you can compare with him." Fellow NL pitcher San Diego Padres reliever Goose Gossage called Gooden "probably the best young player I've seen in nineteen years." In a 3-1 victory over the American League, Gooden and his mighty arm made his appearance as an All-Star rookie one of the game's great moments.

THE SPEED DEMON

Dramatic catches, powerfully hit balls, and great coaching are all parts of the All-Star tradition. So is base running. Maury Wills provided fans with an exciting example of this at the 1962 All-Star Game in Washington, D.C. Wills stopped at first base after his eighth-inning leadoff single. Then the next batter, Jim Davenport, shot off another single. Wills sprang forward and in a flash had covered the ground between first and second. Touching second, he rounded the base, stopped briefly, then dashed on toward third. Outfielder Rocky Colavito fielded the ball and fired it to second base, where second baseman Billy Moran shot the ball to third baseman Brooks Robinson. But Maury Wills slid into third just before the ball smacked Robinson's glove.

Listening to the roar from the stands, Gooden dropped his glove to his side and smiled dazedly at his National League teammates. Then he turned to the deliriously cheering fans.

To batters and pitchers alike, Gooden looked like a star for the 1980s. One of his victims, Detroit Tigers batter Chet Lemon, described Gooden as being in a class by himself. As he put it, "There's not much you're going to do when a guy throws a 2-2 pitch ninety-five miles an hour on the outside corner." Gooden's National League manager, Paul Owens of the Philadelphia Phillies, said of his pitching star, "He's got

An infield catch by Cal Ripken, Jr.

Brooks Robinson.

Perched on the bag's edge, Wills started off the base when the next batter, Felipe Alou, popped up to Leon Wagner in deep right field. Fans jumped to their feet as Wills sped toward home. Could he beat Wagner's throw? Wills calculated the distance, leaned backward, and began a long slide. As Wagner's throw rifled toward home plate, Wills slid in. When the dust cleared, the umpire waved his hands and declared Wills safe.

Maury Wills had scored the third and last National League run in a 3-1 NL victory. His teammates flocked around him and clapped him on the back. The stadium rang with cheers as Wills and his jubilant teammates headed for the dugout.

In the 1962 season, Wills stole 104 bases and won the National League's Most Valuable Player award. But nothing was more exciting than the thrill he gave Washington baseball fans in one of the All-Star Game's greatest moments.

Wills slid under John Romane's tag to score the winning run in the 1962 All-Star Game.

MISSAUKEE DISTRICT LIBRARY

J 796.357 Pot
Potts, Steve, 1956-
All-Star Game
31781

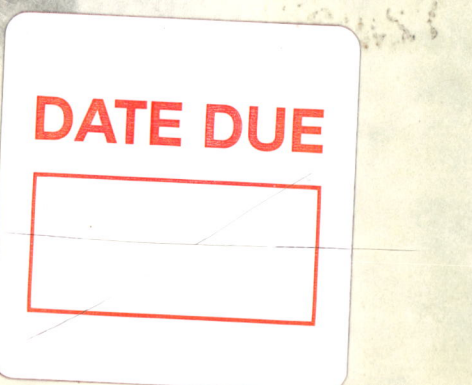

MISSAUKEE DISTRICT LIBRARY